O

PRAYERS

"Prayer is the Key to Heaven,
  But Faith unlocks the Door."

"Therefore, I say unto you,
  What things soever ye desire,
  When ye pray, believe that ye
  Receive them, and ye shall have them."
          —Jesus (St. Mark 11:24)

"Prayer is our telephone to God."
          —M.S.H.

"Prayer changes Things."

One Hundred Short

PRAYERS

by May Stafford Hilburn

Macoy Publishing and

Masonic Supply Company

Richmond, Virginia

Printed in the United States of America

To WALTER
     of precious memory

Contents

One Hundred Short
PRAYERS

1.

OUR Father, we ask Thy guidance in the work which we seek to do in this organization. We realize that we are often beset by doubts and cares and that we make mistakes. Give us patience, love, and a willingness to do our duty in this work and to each other. We love our work here. Give us enthusiasm to promote fellowship and goodwill. All this, we ask. Amen.

2.

OUR Dear Heavenly Father, we have closed the pages of our service for the year just past, and are beginning another year of service and of close fellowship. We give Thee praise for our successful accomplishments, and we ask Thy continued leading and watch-care for the year ahead. May we serve Thee faithfully as we work here together, and may the friendship and love we have for each other grow and bear worthy deeds in the coming year. This we pray. Amen.

3.

WE come into Thy presence, O God, with gratitude for all the blessings of life which You have so graciously given to us. We need Your help in every work we attempt to do. May we go forth from this meeting with a feeling of gladness that we have banded ourselves together to work for the good of our organization. May we always be friends, trying to obey Your will. We ask these blessings for Jesus' sake. Amen.

4.

HEAVENLY Father, accept our work, we pray. And may this meeting here reflect the beauty of our service. Our plans are still in the making for this year's work. Give us the benefit of Thy Holy Spirit to see the most important things to be accomplished. As we go forward, may we find a blessing as we work together. Amen.

5.

MOST Merciful Father, from Whom all good things come, we give Thee thanks for Thy special watch-care during the past year. We bow in humble gratitude, remembering the many favors we have received and the many blessings we have enjoyed. At the beginning of a New Year, we ask Thy continued guidance in all that we do and say. May our service to our work be worthy of Your blessings. Lead us, guide us, and bless us. Amen.

6.

Our Father, we begin a New Year's work and help us, we pray, to make it the best year so far in our history. May we never fail to show our love for Thee and for each other as we serve our organization. May we each feel the deep sense of duty that goes with our obligation for service, and may we never fail to do our best. We praise Thee for all past blessings. We thank Thee. Amen.

7.

FATHER of all Creation, we bring this meeting into Your presence, knowing that Your loving care is around us and that Your will for us and this organization is only for good. May all our work here reflect the loving kindness which we have in our hearts for You and all mankind. May Your loving care for us make us careful for others. Amen.

8.

DEAR Heavenly Father, our gratitude for our many countless blessings fills our hearts and makes us want to work together faithfully for the principles of our Order. We meet here to give praise to You, our Father, and to ask for help in doing our work. We know that Your blessings upon us will strengthen and bless not only us, but all who know of our work. With grateful hearts for all past blessings, we give thanks. Amen.

9.

WE pray, Heavenly Father, humbly, and with a heart full of praise, we enter into Thy presence and bow before Thee. We are privileged to live and work together, free and independent. We give Thee thanks for all that we have in America, for all that we, as American citizens, can give to our nation. During the months ahead, may this altar be fully consecrated to Thee and to all whom we serve. And may the spirit of love prevail in our work, now and forever. Amen.

10.

Our Father, Who art in Heaven, we come into Thy presence with loving gratitude, and with supplication, for Thy continued guidance. We are giving thanks today for a free nation, a nation which has been blest in many wonderful ways. We realize that men who trusted and loved Thee have charted the course of our great land. May we, as citizens of this great nation, never forget that Thou art ruler of nations through the minds of people. We ask that our thoughts may reflect all good to our fellowmen. Amen.

11.

DEAR Father of all, and Ruler of the universe, we approach Thy altar and lay our petitions before Thee. History shows that great men have been born in February who served Thee and this great nation in humbleness and in honor of the cause of freedom. They turned to Thee for strength and guidance. Give us the willingness to serve our organization as faithfully as these great heroes who served and saved our land. Guide us in the right paths, we pray. Amen.

12.

Our Father, Author and Finisher of our faith, give us Thy blessing as we go about our daily tasks in our homes and in all other places of service. Bring us here together, eager to report what we have done and to receive with gladness other duties which may be ours to do. Give us grace to accomplish Thy will in every humble task or in greater work for Thee. And may the Spirit of Christ make us humble in our work, and faithful to each other. In His name, we pray. Amen.

13.

ETERNAL God, Father of us all, we come to Thee at this time, grateful for Thy Son Jesus Who gave His life for us and Who arose from the dead to show that death has no power over those who trust in Thee. At this time of resurrection, we ask Thy blessings. We ask that all our shortcomings may be overcome and forgotten and that a new concept of duty, service and brotherly love may fill our hearts. This is our wish during this Holy Season. Hold Thou our hands to give us strength. Lead us in the way we should go. We ask in the name of Thy Son Jesus and our Risen Lord and Saviour. Amen.

14.

Our Father in Heaven, give us loving hearts to serve Thee, and willing hands to do Thy work here in this fraternal organization. Without Thee we have no plan or program for our work. Help us to do the things You would have us do, in a way You would have us do them. Consecrate this room to Thy service. And help us to be Thy children in deed and in truth. Amen.

15.

WE give thanks today, Our Father, that we may come to Thee in faith, believing that our petition will be heard and answered. We praise Thee for Thy compassion and Thy love, for Thy willingness to hear our prayers. Renew our strength as we labor together. Let us realize more fully that in unity there is power. Cover us with Thy protection and give us peace. This, we ask. Amen.

16.

Our Father, Who maketh the seed to grow and the flowers to bloom in due season, we come asking for a deeper appreciation of all the beauty Thy wisdom hath given to the earth. Help us to find beauty and to cultivate love as we walk our chosen way. Give us a song to sing as we work together, and a heart of cheer to bless those who work with us. Amen.

17.

DEAR Father, to Whom we turn in every need, at this time we give Thee our heartfelt devotion, our gratitude and our praise, for all the mercies You have shown to us during the years. With the coming of a new growing season, may our good deeds grow and mature and bloom with beauty as we help each other in our great brotherhood of service. In humble thanksgiving for Thy unfailing love, we give Thee thanks. Amen.

18.

Most Everlasting and Eternal God, at the beginning of the spring season, may we feel the spirit of growth in our organization and see the fruits of our winter's work as progress and advancement. May we sow the flowers of good deeds at this spring planting time, and may our harvest of love be abundant and satisfying. We ask Thy blessing on each one of us. Give us more insight into the meaning of our work. Amen.

19.

FATHER of us all, we ask for loving hearts to better serve the cause of humanity. Help us to see the needs of our less fortunate brothers and sisters, and give us spiritual insight to know how to help their needs. This is a season of preparation for a bountiful harvest. It is time to sow if we are to reap. Help us to sow kindness as we work to do Thy will here in this organization. Amen.

20.

HEAVENLY Father, with reverence we come at this time, asking only for the manifestation of Thy love, and the opportunity to reflect Thy love, in our work here together. Help us to promote goodwill and give unselfish service. Accept the work of our hands as the true offering of our hearts. Amen.

21.

Our Father, we pray for Thy blessing as we come together to work for our common cause. Help us to search our hearts for our real motive. To find out if we work for praise, or from a sense of duty, or for love. If any selfishness controls us, help us rid ourselves of it. Instill within us a desire to please Thee, doing our best always. Amen.

22.

OUR Dear Heavenly Father, with grateful hearts, we again seek Thy presence knowing that from Thee comes our strength, our success in our work. May we ever be faithful to our high calling in this fine fraternal organization. Founded on the principles of faith, may we each fulfill our vows as we work with each other. Only by working together in harmony can we find a satisfaction in our work. Help us to attain our purpose. We ask in the name of Jesus Christ, our Lord. Amen.

23.

OUR Beloved and Gracious Heavenly Father, Thou Who holds the world in Thy powerful and loving hands, give us the vision to see that our patriotic service is an attribute to God and Country, equal to service on the battlefield or in any line of consecrated effort. Within the walls of this room we come to do faithfully and well that to which we have pledged ourselves. We ask Thy blessings on our land, our people, our flag, and for all it means to be a free people. Humbly, we bring our petitions to Thy throne. Amen.

24.

Our Father, the earth is beautiful with the flowers Thy love caused to grow everywhere. Help us to grow the flowers of love in all our service to Thee. May the beauty of Thy service bloom into flowers of great fragrance and may people everywhere recognize as we teach the principles of our fraternity that Thy guiding hand has led us into the path of service. Amen.

25.

ETERNAL God, today we are come to pay a loving tribute to the memory of our brave soldiers—men and women who have given their lives for the defense of our Country. Their service for our great Nation helped to make this land safe for all of us to worship as we choose, to serve, to live, to be free. May their hallowed memory inspire us to give our best wherever we may be called to serve. Amen.

26.

OUR Heavenly Father, Creator and Ruler of the Universe, our hearts are humbled before Thee. Grant, O Father, that we may realize and appreciate Thy love more fully and that we may be inspired to serve Thee wherever we are and in whatever we do. Give us faith and love, we pray. Amen.

✝

27.

FATHER of all, to Whom we pray, lead us, guide us, and help us to find Thy glory in everything we do. Help us to see that to serve faithfully and well is pleasing in Thy sight. Help us to find happiness in every duty we undertake. To Thee we now give all honor and praise, and gratitude for Thy care and protection. Amen.

28.

Our Father, we bow our heads at this time in gratitude for all the blessings we have received from Thee. We are an honored nation in a great company of nations. Our Flag stands for all that is noble and true in word and in deed. May we be stirred with pride as we gaze upon its beautiful colors of red, white and blue, and may our love for our Flag grow with each year of our lives. May Flag Day to us mean a closer walk with Thee and with each other. Amen.

29.

GRACIOUS Lord, today we come honoring Thee with a pledge anew for service to God and home and native land. Our Flag of the Free is a gift of our faith. It is an answer to our prayers for a God-fearing land. Direct our lives, help us to do the right as found in Thy precepts. Grace and strength is a gift from Thee and, knowing this, we cannot be afraid. Bless and keep us, we pray. Amen.

30.

Our Heavenly Father, we ask Thy continued guidance. Without Thy leading, our path would be rough and hard to find. Be with us, lead us, help us to reflect Thy love. Bless our Nation. Put it in the hearts of our people to honor our flag, to assist our leaders, to humbly give Thee thanks for this great land. And to Thee belongs all the honor and the glory, forever. Amen.

31.

Our Father, we come into Thy presence bringing our work to Thee, asking a blessing, making a vow to serve Thee faithfully. We offer the love of our hearts to Thee, and ask Thee to bless the work of our hands for the kingdom. Help us to find peace in our daily lives. Give us comfort in our sorrows. Amen.

32.

Our Father which art in Heaven, we come bringing this meeting into Thy sanctuary, praying for Thy help in making our work a blessing unto Thee. We need vision to more clearly see the beauty of the work to which we have been called. Help us to plant the seed and till the soil for a bountiful harvest of good deeds. Amen.

33.

Father of us all, be with us in our work at this time. Give us grace and love for all that we find to do. May we realize that each task is a part of the whole work. And each doing his best will make a fine result in fraternity. Be our strength and our guide. Amen.

34.

Iᴛ is with grateful hearts, our Heavenly Father, that we bow before Thee today, giving thanks for the freedom that we enjoy. We are a nation, under God, which is pledged to honor and truth. Our ancestors gave us this nation, defended by brave men who gave their lives to establish the United States of America. We give Thee thanks for our heritage. We ask Thy help that we, as patriots, may never falter in our duty to preserve our nation. And to Thee be the honor and the glory. Amen.

35.

ALMIGHTY God, Guardian of our lives and Ruler of our destiny, we give Thee thanks for our beautiful homeland, our great nation, founded by free men who wanted always to be free. We give Thee praise for Thy leading under the laws Thou hast set for the founding of freedom. We ask Thy continued watch-care. And may our beautiful flag, the symbol of freedom, be an inspiration also to all the oppressed nations of the earth who are seeking freedom. Amen.

36.

Oᴜʀ Father, our nation celebrates the birth of its freedom in this month. May we, as free people, realize that brave men and women years ago resolved to be free and because of that we stand free today to work, to serve, to worship. May we together, here, find greater plans for service to our organization because we are a free people. Give us grace and strength to dignify our work for Thee. We ask Thy continued protection. Amen.

37.

Lᴏʀᴅ God of all, this is the month we give thanks for brave men and women who more than two hundred years ago were willing to give their lives to make our nation a nation of free men and women. We thank Thee for our great heritage of freedom and we pray now for freedom for all nations and all people. May our actions, our deeds, and our words show to others that a true spirit of freedom prevails only from Thy grace and by unselfish service according to Thy ways. Give us grace and strength as we work for Thee and for each other. May our Flag of Freedom be in our hearts, now and forever. Amen.

38.

MERCIFUL Father, forgive us if we have neglected to do our duty to Thee and to each other. We come into Thy presence asking Thy blessing on all we say and do here. May our meeting bring good that is far-reaching and effective for Thy honor and glory. Amen.

39.

FATHER of all mankind, we approach Thy altar with a prayer of gratitude for a year that has found it a peaceful nation as well as a Christian nation. Our service to Thee is part of our lives. We turn to Thee in times of distress and dismay, asking for protection. In times of prosperity and success we need to give Thee thanks for Thy protecting love. Give us larger vision, more eager hearts to do Thy will here in this organization as well as in our daily lives. We need Thee more each day as we meet the difficulties of life. Cover us with Thy protecting wing, keep us safe. Amen.

40.

Oᴜʀ Father, we enter Thy presence with gratitude and praise. We know that by recognizing You as our Heavenly Father, we can find our way better and serve mankind more faithfully. We, in our organization here, have certain duties to perform and obligations to carry out. We pray for Thy guiding hand to help us do all things to Thy glory. Amen.

41.

Our Dear Heavenly Father, we approach Thy throne with gratitude for the blessings which have been ours for many years. May we never forget that Thou art the Author and the Finisher of our faith. May we serve Thee faithfully in our work here. And may we love each other with the same unselfish love with which you have loved us. We thank Thee for all good things. Amen.

42.

GOD of our fathers, Forgiver of our sins, we pray Thy blessings on all mankind. May the light of freedom shine into the hearts of men until the whole world is free to worship Thee in spirit and in truth. May they seek Thee as we seek Thee, now, in humbleness and in faith. Give us grateful hearts for the blessed heritage of Thy love which Thy Son Jesus came on earth to bring. For His sake we ask, and pray in His name. Amen.

43.

Our Father, we realize that to be called upon to serve in any place is an honor and a privilege. We also know that work half done is a shame that falls upon us all. Help us to give our best service to the smallest duty as well as to the larger task. With Thy help we can work and not grow weary. We pray for the strength of Thy arm to lean upon. Amen.

44.

DEAR Heavenly Father, this summer's work will soon draw to a close. The autumn will take the place of summer and, with the passing of the weeks, we will begin to look for the harvest of our work. We have had many duties and problems, and have given thought to the work in many ways. And through it all we have enjoyed the meeting with each other. Sisters in a common cause, workers for the good of all, we give thanks. Go with us when we leave this room. Bring us safely back to work together again. Amen.

45.

Our Father, it is the beginning of the harvest season. Those who have planted loving kindness are reaping loving kindness in return. We know the law of love can solve all difficulties. Give us contrite hearts, give us forgiving minds. Help us to harvest loving kindness. Bless us and keep us, we pray. Amen.

46.

HEAVENLY Father, we approach the harvest of our sowing knowing that some of the seed we have sown has not produced the benefits we had hoped for, but we pray for courage to weed out the mistakes. Show us the way to plow deeper and till the ground of service more thoroughly. We meet here as workers in a common cause trying to live daily the things we strive to teach. May our efforts result in stronger friendships and closer ties to each other. Amen.

47.

OUR Gracious Heavenly Father, we praise Thee for the many blessings which have been given to us. Our harvest of grain throughout our nation will be more than we need. We thank Thee for the opportunity of sharing our bounty with those who have little. May the love which You have given to our people help us to show love to those who need it. And give us grace to do Thy will. Amen.

48.

HEAVENLY Father, it is time for the harvest, the reaping of the grain we have scattered. If we have failed in our duties, if neglect has been our fault, we pray Thee to give us strength to do better in the coming year. Bless those who have learned to love our work and to love Thee. Amen.

49.

Our Loving Father, we thank Thee for life and health and strength, for work to do and the will to do it, for the friendships we have found in our association with each other, for the kindness and genuine goodness we recognized as we worked together. We thank Thee for all these blessings, and for each one who has become a dedicated channel for Thy love. Bless each one, we pray. Amen.

50.

HEAVENLY Father, our shelter in times of stress, the winter days are just ahead. May the love in our hearts keep us warm, willing to serve, grateful for giving and sharing all that we have, and hope that we may meet around this altar for many years to come. It is with full realization, we acknowledge that all of our blessings were given from Thy loving hand. We ask that our service to our neighbors may be counted worthy. And to Thee, we give the glory. Amen.

51.

OUR Most Gracious and Loving Father, as we approach the last months of our year, may we look back and not be ashamed of our work here. May we find we have been faithful to Thee and to each other. We ask Thy continued blessing, now and for the days ahead. Amen.

closing
the end of our meeting tonight

our work here.

52.

Our Father, Giver of all good gifts, hear us now as we pray. The harvest is gathered, the year will soon be done. We bring our love and our service to Thee, and hope we have done a good work and that it is pleasing in Thy sight. In the months ahead, may we find peace and happiness in serving each other better. Amen.

53.

Our Gracious Heavenly Father, with thanksgiving and praise for Thy loving kindness, we bow before Thee. Thou hast been a loving Father from generation to generation, willing to accept man's petitions when they came in faith. At this time, in faith, we bring as our offering of love, the work we are now doing, serving with gladness. Bless us, we pray. Amen.

54.

Our Father, Lord of Hosts and King of Kings, we, Thy children, approach Thy throne with gratitude for Thy mercy. Thy loving heart has room, and to spare, for all who worship and adore Thee. Give us grace to serve all mankind, faith to discern hidden good, love to overlook unkindness, and may we be merciful to those who have not learned Thy righteousness. Amen.

55.

Our Heavenly Father, Author and Finisher of our faith, give us a vision of loving service, of honest effort, to bring before Thee. May we ever remember that we are Thy children as we serve each other, and as we serve Thee. Be with us in all we say and do, in faith, with love. This, we pray. Amen.

56.

WE come before Thee, Heavenly Father, bearing our sheaves at this Thanksgiving time, laying our offering upon Thy altar, asking that Thy love may find beauty in what we have done in Thy name. All over our land, people kneel, bringing an offering of love. To those whose gift is only love, whose sheaves were a disappointment to them, let them see that love for Thee is the greatest gift of all. For in loving Thee, we learn to love one another. Bless our work, help us to come close to Thee as we go forth to labor. Amen.

57.

GRACIOUS Father, Who knows our actions and the intentions of our heart, we come to bring humble thanks for this Thanksgiving Season. We have had a prosperous year. We have been divinely blest. Keep us close to Thee, Father, and give us a realization of our blessings. Our nation is at peace. We are the benefactor of hungry people. For all these blessings we praise Thee, our Father, Ruler of the Heavens and of the Earth. Amen.

58.

Our Dear Father, at this approaching Thanksgiving Season, we bow before Thee in gratitude and praise. Free people, in a peaceful land, we come in humbleness to Thy throne, offering our harvest of love and good deeds as our gift. Our hearts are grateful, our hopes for future work greater than ever. We ask Thy guidance. Bless us and keep us. This, we ask. Amen.

59.

O Gracious Lord in Heaven, with thanksgiving we approach Thy throne. Remembering the early pilgrims of our land who gave thanks for Thy protection during their first days alone in a strange land, we give thanks for their courage, their faith in safety under Thy protection and care. Give us that faith as we look into another year which will soon be here. Thy blessings we ask in all we do. Amen.

60.

Our Father, we give thanks for each person belonging to our fraternal order who recognizes that our work is founded upon Thy everlasting word. This kinship has become a mighty force for good, reflecting Thy holiness, giving beauty and truth wherever found, and showing Thy purpose for mankind's advancement. As we serve Thee through the teachings of the Holy Word, may our own lives reflect the beauty of Thy grace. Amen.

61.

Oᴜʀ Father, it is a holy gift You gave us long ago when Jesus, Your only Son, was sent to earth to teach men about Your great love. Because He came, the world has found a great light. Our hearts know what love really means. His life is the pattern for all goodness, all holiness. We thank You for this great gift of love. Hold us in the hollow of Your hand until our service is over, our life is done. And to You be the honor and glory and praise, for Jesus' sake. Amen.

62.

DEAR Father of us all, we approach
the end of the year with hopes that our
stewardship has been acceptable to Thee
and to each other. May the coming years
bring our work to a fuller realization of
Thy love. We know that with Thee to
help and to guide, we cannot fail. Bless us,
we pray. Lead us, we ask. Amen.

63.

HEAVENLY Father, Thy altar is our meeting place at this time. May the gift of Thy love which came in the form of Thy Son, be in each heart as we work together. Thy gift to us brought blessings that cannot be measured in words. Our lives have been made better because He came. Our work here reflects the love and forgiveness He came to teach. We give thanks for Thy love which sent Jesus to earth to bring us peace. Bless us as we work together. For His Name's sake. Amen.

64.

BLESSED Heavenly Father, we meet to give thanks and to worship Thy Son Who came into the world to teach us how to live closer to Thee. At this Christmas Season, may we see in each helpless child the Holy Child Who was born in a manger and Whose life transformed the world. May each glowing candle reflect our love for Him, may each Christmas song give forth the harmony that comes from serving Him with our whole heart. May we enter the New Year with greater faith, holier purpose, and deeper friendships, to go forth to love and to serve humanity. This we ask in Jesus' name. Amen.

65.

LOVING and Forgiving God, our Father, our dwelling place in times of stress and sorrow, we come, knowing Thy love enfolds all who seek Thee. We are closing the pages of the year and we ask Thy forgiveness for some wrinkled blotted pages in the record. Our grief at duties half-done, work neglected, and prayers unsaid can be blotted out only by Thy love. Forgive us, Father, we pray Thee, and give us another chance. Amen.

66.

Oᴜʀ Father, we come into Thy presence at this hour, asking Thy blessing upon our plans and activities during the coming year. We are looking forward for increased enthusiasm, faithfulness and loyalty to our obligations, our duties, and to each other. With Thy help we shall accomplish much for the benefit of our fraternal order and our community. We thank Thee for blessings which have been given to us in past years of our service. We ask Thy help in all we do and say, for the uplifting of faith and love in the year we are now entering. Help us to make our obligations sacred to Thee and to each member. Bring us together in a spirit of love always. Amen.

67.

OUR Dear Heavenly Father, with humble hearts we approach Thy throne to offer a pledge of faithfulness. We pledge to perform all the duties of the offices into which we are to be installed. We promise faithful attendance during the year, and we pledge to Thee our honest efforts to do our work so as to honor Thee, in every action we take. Accept our thanks for the opportunity we find here to serve each other. In the name of Thy Son Jesus, we make our pledge to fulfill our obligations. Amen.

68.

WE come into Thy presence today, our Loving Heavenly Father, knowing that our work is necessary to the promotion of our organization. We, who have been chosen to fill the offices of this group, come in humbleness to kneel at Thy altar, and to give thanks for Thy help. May each duty we undertake be done with good faith, and may we find comfort in happiness in that which we do. We ask Thy continued blessing. Amen.

69.

DEAR Heavenly Father, Creator and Guardian of mankind, we ask Thy favor and Thy blessing. We have pledged ourselves to do a certain work for our organization and for Thee. In the days ahead we may lack wisdom to do this work for Thy glory. We pray for enlightenment to perform in a trustworthy way and we ask for patience and fortitude as we go about our several tasks. Help us and keep us, we pray. Amen.

70.

Our Heavenly Father, Creator and Ruler of our lives, we have come tonight, members and officers of our two organizations, to pledge ourselves for another year's work. We thank Thee for the opportunity given us to work together for the betterment of our membership, our community, and our great nation. We thank Thee for the meaning of our pledge, our obligations, our cooperation in work that is our part of fraternal service during the coming year. We work together in gladness, mindful of the strength that working together brings. May we each feel the responsibility of our work, and may the fact that we serve each other make us better servants for every good cause we sponsor. We ask Thy watchcare as we go forward. Amen.

71.

O<small>UR</small> Father, tonight we have met for an especial purpose. We are here to pledge ourselves for another year's work in Thy name, and for the advancement of every fraternal enterprise our two great organizations strive to do. It is good for us to hold this joint session. It makes us mindful of the fact that by working together, we increase our strength, our faith in our work, and our happiness in our fine cooperation. We know that under Thy guidance we can find added blessings. Help us to give our best service to the things our orders teach. Together, we can lift many a load; together, we can find happiness and peace. As we pledge ourselves, may we feel Thy loving presence. Amen.

72.

ALMIGHTY God, in Whose name we pledge ourselves to our work, we meet together tonight, brothers and sisters, in a great cause—that of serving wherever we are called to give help and strength. It is good for us to meet together like we are doing now. We have a feeling of unity in our association, a feeling of cooperation that makes our work twice as beneficial. We know that in working together, we may find new vision of greater work for ourselves and for Thee. We ask Thee to bless every good work we undertake. We seek Thy help in our efforts to help each other, and ask for the blessing that comes from work well done. May we all together march forward to greater deeds, greater opportunities to serve. We are ever mindful of Thy love. For all this we give thanks. Amen.

73.

Our Father, on this most special occasion, we come before Thee asking Thy blessing upon our joint meeting here tonight. We have come to pledge ourselves for another year's work in each of our organizations, doing Thy will as best we can, serving each other and giving faithful work in the positions to which we have been elected. Our mutual interests have brought us together. Our mutual teachings of the brotherhood of man and the sisterhood of woman make us dependent on each other. Together, we can better serve; together, we gain strength; and, without each other, we would fail in a measure, to do our best work. It is good for brothers and sisters to work together in unity. It makes us stronger. We ask Thy blessing. Amen.

74.

HEAVENLY Father, our refuge and our support in times of need, we bring our year's work to a close and ask Thy blessing on the things we have tried to do. We ask that we be given another chance to finish that which we have left undone. May the coming year reflect our humility of spirit and loving service, that must be found in all acceptable work. Give us grace and strength. Give us courage to face the future with a grateful heart and a willing mind. Enfold us in Thy love, cover us with Thy protecting care. Amen.

75.

$\mathcal{D}$EAR Father, we have met to observe our _____ anniversary. We can look back upon the years with pride, giving thanks for the progress we have made, for the work we have accomplished. We know that Thy hand has guided us, Thy love inspired us, Thy watch-care shielded us. For all this we now offer our grateful thanks. In the years to come, keep us doing our work with gratitude that we may continue to be successful. And may Thy love continue to bless us, we pray. Amen.

76.

Most Gracious Heavenly Father, we thank Thee for this food which has been prepared for the nourishment of our physical bodies. Bless each one here as we come together in fellowship. Give us patience, love, and willingness to do our duty to this work, and to each other. We pray that our faith may be strengthened, and our love increased, and our Christian service continued. Give us enthusiasm to promote fellowship and goodwill and we ask that Thou will sustain us in our every need. Amen.

77.

ETERNAL God, Father of us all, as we approach the Easter Season we are reminded of Thy great love which sent Thy only begotten Son down to earth to bring salvation to us all. We thank Thee for His pure sinless life given in sacrifice for us. In humility, we think of His death on the cross and the glory of His resurrection. Our Father, accept our love, our obedience, and our service. We give it to Thee in the name of Jesus Christ, our Lord. Amen.

78.

Our Heavenly Father, it is with joy and gladness that we come to dedicate this _____ for Thy service. It is a gift of love from _____. We ask Thy blessing on the givers and we give thanks that we have been the recipients. May all we say and do here, at this time, and in times to come, reflect to Thy honor and glory. May we ever be conscious of our closeness to Thee and may our service, as well as this gift of love, be acceptable in Thy sight. Amen.

(If given by the speaker, change second and third sentences to:)
It is a gift of love from us who have been called to service in this especial place and for a special work. We ask Thy blessing upon the gift and we give thanks that we are allowed to be the givers.

79.

Our Father, we ask Thy blessing on all who have been chosen to chart the course of our great nation. In whatever capacity each one serves, be the work great or seemingly unimportant, may each give his best, knowing that his place needs to meet the test of loyalty and faith if the purpose of our government is to be accomplished. When we read the history of our republic, we know that if our leaders through the years had not trusted Thy divine direction we would not have attained freedom and remained free. Hold us in Thy protection, keep us a Christian Nation. Without Thy guiding hand, our road may become obscure. We ask Thy blessing on all those who serve. Amen.

80.

HEAVENLY Father, today we honor the flag of our beloved land. We bow in prayer to thank You for its meaning, its beauty, its inspiration to us, a free people. Its blue field of honor reminds us that we give to You honor and praise in everything we do. Its bright stars mean loyalty to our land and to You, the Guardian and Protector of our great nation. You gave to us the ability and the desire to live honorably and to loyally serve our unfortunate brothers. Our flag's white bars of purity and the red of hero's blood, give us courage and faith. Bless our beloved flag and keep our country safe, forever, we pray. Amen.

81.

OUR Heavenly Father, we ask Your blessing on all the world and especially on the men who are fathers in great lands and in lands we do not know. May every child give honor to his father, as Your only begotten Son gave honor to You while He was here on earth. And may every father give faithful love to his own children and help serve little children who have no father. We ask a blessing on our great land whose men have marched forth to defend and protect our homes. And may we have a deeper love for You, the Father of us all. Amen.

82.

Our Father, Who art in Heaven, bless, we pray, the young fathers of our broad land who, today, are leading our children. Give them the wisdom to train and teach the little ones who will be the leaders of tomorrow. And inspire the fathers of today with courage and faith so that future generations may love their land and its free people and honor Thee, their God. Amen.

83.

Our Heavenly Father, bless, we pray, the fathers who have trained and led their children in paths of faith and duty, and who now remember the days of their youth. Hold their hands, Father, and listen to their petitions. The road behind them is longer than the road ahead. Hold them close, protect them, and let the light of Thy love guide them forever. Amen.

84.

Our Father, with gratitude, we come to You, giving thanks for all the many blessings which You have given to us. We thank You for the blessing of good mothers, and for men and women who can look back upon their childhood and remember a loving and kind mother who taught them in the right way. We pray that we, who are mothers now, may be as faithful, as loyal, and as kind as our mothers. And may we so live that our children will look back upon our lives and say, "Thank You, God, for my good and faithful mother." We ask this blessing. Amen.

85.

O Thou wise and understanding God, we ask Thy blessing for all mothers, everywhere. For the young mother with this new experience of motherhood which will bring many problems through the years. She will need wisdom and judgment. We ask Thee to show her the way she should go. We ask Thy blessing on the mother who has finished her work of rearing and training her children; for those who now look back upon their fruitful years, who have only memories of children around their knee. Help the mothers of our land to teach children in the right way so that the memories of the past will be happy ones without regret for neglected duties. Amen.

86.

GOD BLESS THE MOTHERS

God bless the mothers, everywhere,
Who bow with humble hearts in prayer,
Who seek Thy help, to know Thy will,
Their work of mothers to fulfill.
Who teach Thy love to children small,
Teach Thy protection over all.
Renew their strength and give them grace
To stand within their sacred place.
Oh, walk with them; they need to know
The path Thy love would have them go.
God bless the weary, tired ones,
Who serve their daughters and their sons
In a thousand uncomplaining ways
On prayerful nights and hurried days,
Whose tender love, through ill or good,
Like God's own love, misunderstood.
Oh, bless and keep within Thy care
The faithful mothers, everywhere.

87.

OUR Father, in Jesus' name we pray, asking that Thy love and protection be around _____ who is very ill. We come to Thee asking that _____ be restored to health and strength, according to Thy wisdom and Thy will, and that we all may learn the lesson to be found in this affliction. Give us faith to know that according to Thy promises all things work for good to all who love and trust Thee. Bless the worried loved ones who join in this prayer, and give them the comfort of Thy love. Amen.

88.

O Loving and Compassionate Saviour,
humbly, we come to petition for the heal-
ing of _____ who is chained to the bed
of illness. If it be Thy will may he be re-
leased by the power of Thy love. Speak
the word to heal and restore, and to banish
all pain. In faith, we come asking. Amen.

89.

O God, our Father, to Whom we come in these days of illness and sorrow, we ask Thy mercy and especial loving watch and care over this one we so dearly love. Be with her during these days when she needs Thee so very much. Help her to feel Thy love, give her strength in her body and faith in her heart to know that with Thy strong tender arms to hold her, she need have no fear. And at night, give her peaceful, refreshing sleep. This, we pray. Amen.

90.

DEAR Father, Giver of all good gifts, Healer of broken hearts, we ask Thy comforting love now, when we have come to pay a last tribute to a beloved one. Give us the consolation to know that death is not the end, but that after the Spirit has discarded the garment used on earth, the glorified robes of eternity will be given to our beloved and that we, too, shall wear such garments when we have laid down this mortal body. Give us a hope and an assurance that we shall meet where there is no parting, no sickness, and no sorrow. Bless us, keep us, and Thine be the glory forever. Amen.

91.

DEAR Father of us all, there are days when trials seem to beset us, and we struggle to be free from disappointment and daily care. Help us, we pray, to accept the day's work and do it well. Give us a song to sing as we work, and a hope for Thy approval to cheer us along life's way. So often we forget that Thy hand is ever near to guide us. And, in our own feeble strength, we strive to do the hard way what, with Thy help, would be easy and joyful. We need Thy guiding hand, Thy divine wisdom to do our best. Bless us, and to Thee will we give all honor, all praise. Amen.

92.

DEAR Father, we ask for strength and faith and willing hearts to study well the lessons of life which we must learn. We need spiritual strength which creates faith. Give us Thy blessing of grace to trust Thee for our needs. Keep our feet from stumbling and help us to walk with confidence as we lovingly serve Thee. Help us to find the purpose of our life and give us the ability to show Thy love for all people as part of our work for Thee. In humility, we bow before Thee; in love, we offer ourselves for Thy leading. Amen.

93.

HEAVENLY Father, we, Thy children, pray for those today who need Thy protecting care. Guide those whose paths are not clearly defined and bring a faith to them which will give them courage to walk an unknown way. Help them to not be afraid to hold Thy hand and walk in the dark until their vision clears and they can see the path which they have come was given to them because of Thy unfailing love. Comfort their loneliness, console them and bring to their hearts the benediction of peace, we pray. Amen.

94.

Our Father, we know that coming to Thee brings peace to our hearts. We know that doubt and despair will vanish when, in faith, we lay our cares upon the altar of Thy love. We have proved Thy promises over and over, and have rejoiced to find them always true. Help us to remember that faith unlocks the door to Thy presence and that we can approach and find Thee at anytime, at any hour, and at any place. Help us to realize that we are never alone, that always Thou art with us if we but turn and seek Thy protection and comforting love. For this we give Thee praise forever. Amen.

95.

OUR Father, to Whom we come in times of joy as well as in times of distress, help us, serving together, to know the blessing of Thy gracious approval. May we each feel the glow of happiness that comes with harmonious endeavor. Renew our energy if we grow careless or weary, and help us to progress day by day in Faith and Understanding and in Love. If it rains discouragement, help us to see behind the temporary clouds the bright sunshine of an accomplished work, of a fitting service, of a better understanding of our necessary labor. Give us Thy continued leading, we pray. Amen.

96.

GRACIOUS Father, Thy love surrounds us as we bow to give Thee thanks. We come in faith believing that our work is part of Thy divine plan for service to mankind. Our work is consecrated to Thee and to Thy kingdom. Our secret motives are known to Thee. If we have allowed selfishness to creep into our hearts, if we are serving for self-glory in any way, purge us clean and make our service acceptable. May each of us carry his own part of the work, not shifting or turning aside, but with firm purpose standing faithful, serving to the end. We pray in humbleness and with deep sincerity. Amen.

97.

FATHER of all, Ruler of Heaven and Earth, we approach Thy throne, bringing our gifts to lay before Thee. Our purpose has been to serve willingly, joyfully, knowing that Thy will for us is to do our best. Our love, our hopes went into all we did. We pray that our gifts of love and our hope may receive Thy blessings. Amen.

98.

FATHER of us all, bring into this room, now, the realization of our many blessings. May we recognize that what we have done has been to promote fellowship and a better understanding of people and places. Bless our efforts to serve; forgive anything we have failed to do. And be our shield and our strength, we pray. Amen.

99.

Our Father, through the centuries, men have turned to Thee in earnest supplication, offering themselves to Thee for Thy service. Some have been called to great deeds and their lips have been touched with fire as they gave their inspired messages. Others have served in what appeared to be unimportant places and have often stood alone, unnoticed, unpraised, but they served faithfully, doing their work for the glory of God. We ask an especial blessing on these who stand, a lonely guard, in their appointed places. Brighten the spots where they are, we pray, and give them a great joy for having done all for Thy dear sake. Amen.

100.

HEAVENLY Father, Ruler of heaven and earth, we humbly come, asking Thy pardon for our sins of omission. In our weakness, or our forgetfulness, we have failed to do the work we set out to do. We ask Thy forgiveness, and we seek Thy blessing, Thy continued love; give us strength when we are weak. When we doubt, give us the joy of renewed faith. Stir within our hearts an eagerness to serve Thee better. And, at the close of each day, before we sleep, accept our petition for continued courage and faith. And to Thee, we give all honor and glory. Amen.